Contents

INTRODUCTION	1
Chapter 1	2
Chapter 2	7
Chapter 3	10
Chapter 4	12
Chapter 5	14
Chapter 6	18
Chapter 7	19
Chapter 8	21
Chapter 9	24
Chapter 10	26
CONCLUSION	28

INTRODUCTION

If you do a random sampling or conduct a research and ask people of their major goals and objectives in life, they would probably give you a straight answer, such as, "I want to be successful, travel round the world, be happy, have a good job," These are all wishes or dreams and none of them are clear goals, there is a saying that, *"A goal that is not written down is nothing more than a wish."*, a wish is not connected to a plan of action.

As you write out your goals, you will quickly see how specific they are.

When you create a goal, you want to focus on it and work toward achieving it;.

As a project manager I subjected myself to thorough planning and developmental schemes, I set target for myself on personal development every week with a goal of better me both in institution of learning and working sites.

This book will guide us through ways of setting and accomplishing our goals in all ramification of life, Strategic planning is a critical activity for any goal to be accomplished.

After reading this book someone will find a reason to be encouraged; this book is a tool for allowing us to discover ourselves through all accomplished achievements

Goals are more deliberate than desires and momentary intentions. Therefore, setting goals means that a person has committed thought, emotion, and behavior towards attaining the goal.

Chapter 1

SET GOALS

According to Dictionary, A *goal* is an objective or target that someone is trying to reach or achieve. *Goal* is also the end point of a race. A *goal* is an aim or objective that you work toward with effort and determination.

Goals are more deliberate than desires and momentary intentions. Therefore, setting goals means that a person has committed thought, emotion, and behavior towards attaining the goal.

Goals are broad statements of where someone or organization would like to see itself in the future. Goals are more targeted to specific areas of action, Goals are supported by objectives, which are measurable.

A goal is a desire, intention, purpose, ambition, aspiration in which the aim or object towards which an endeavor, efforts and trial is directed

The starting point for any strategic plan is the development of effective and actionable goals and objectives

Importance of Goals
Goals are important because they can provide a clear sense of direction to guide employee behavior, help measure the level of success across individuals and teams, and they can even be motivating or inspiring when certain kinds of goals are set. But

most importantly, goals can unite team members and teams toward a common purpose.

- Setting goals helps trigger new behaviors,
- helps guides your focus
- helps you sustain that momentum in life
- Goals Help You Stay Motivated.
- Setting Goals Keeps You Accountable.

There are different types of *goals.*
- SMART goals
- Foundational and life time goals.
- Career goals.
- Professional development goals.
- Financial goals
- Educational goals

SMART goals;

Specific

Measurable

Attainable

Relevant

Time based

A goal must be able to work through these five important key words; Setting a SMART goal will help you understand exactly what you need to do (and when you need to do it) to achieve your desired outcome.

Specific Goals Specific goals specifically indicate what you need to accomplish also all about *the Details of your desire ·* what you want to accomplish, attain or realize·

Goals that are specific, clear expectations. What do you want to accomplish? What's the purpose of the goal? Are there any limitations or perceived obstacles or other requirements to keep in mind?

Specific goals must be clearly defined, identified, and definite with precised objectives, Goals that are specific have a great chance of being accomplished, Parameters must be set on what you want to achieve also how and when to achieve it

Measurable goals means that you identify exactly what it is you will see, hear and feel when you reach your goal. It means breaking your goal down into measurable elements.

Assessing progress helps you to stay focused, meet your deadlines, and feel the excitement of getting closer to achieving your goal.

Attainable goals; The goal should be attainable Achievable: Attainable and not impossible to achieve. is the goal realistic? Can it be achieved within the time frame given? Within reach, realistic, and relevant to your life purpose. Always have the believe that your goals are achievable; Make sure your goal is reasonable.

Relevant; A goal must be relevant to your capabilities and growth potential, the goal must aligns with the plans and purpose to be accomplished

Career goals; Career goals are targets towards your aspirations of what you want to become in life professionally, the position you want to attain, this is a statement that explains how you plan to progress in your career, your personal vision and mission for the proposed future of your career

Financial goals; Most financial goals is saving enough money life fulfillment and retirement, a personal financial goal should have timeline, this could be a long or short term

To fulfill financial goals;

Save for retirement
Invest in bonds, shares
Run away from debt
Improve your growth mindset.
Know your spending limits
Make yourself financially independent
Have confidence in your money management

Health and Fitness Goals
The most important goal in life should be to stay alive and healthy. When you are fit physically and mentally, you will find it easier to function well in other areas. Take charge of your health by making conscious decisions to be healthy and this also comprises the wellness of emotional, intellect, social, economic, spiritual and other areas of life.

Here are some health goals you can set for yourself:

To enjoy excellent health.
To live a long life.
Keep a regular workout regimen.
Start eating a vegetarian diet.
Sleep eight hours a night.
Set and go to regular health checkups and screenings for generational health concerns.
Seek routine therapy or counseling to improve and maintain mental health

Some fitness goals

Shedding fat – The single most common goal of the people who decide to start exercising is their desire to lose fat or weight

Building muscles – Some people don't have a weight problem but just want to build muscles.

Professional development goals; these are objectives you can set for yourself to help further your career. These might include taking steps to learn relevant skills, expand your professional network, or find more satisfaction at work. the reasons for choosing the field you have chosen, is a written description of your long-term professional objectives. Setting goals for professional development is an important part of advancing your career.

Develop a statement of purpose
Always ask for feedback
Have a timeline for every milestone
Let the goals be specific and be Measurable
You must have a starting point and destination
Evaluate your past experience and identify some natural skills you possess
Identify what so ever that motivates you about your carrier

Learning goals/ Educational goals

These goals are all about the new skills and abilities you learn and how you can use them moving forward. Learning goals open up new opportunities. At the end of the year, you can reflect on them and use them to help build your plans for the future.

It usually involves identifying objectives, choosing attainable short-term goals and then creating a plan for achieving those goals. Defining what must be learned and how to accomplish the goals sets a foundation for effective learning, remember that your personal educational aspirations will becoming a reality much faster and easier when stated as an educational goal.

By all these stated goals you will;

Become an inspiration to others
Master your skills
Double your personal income
Get promoted

Chapter 2

HAVE A GAME PLAN

A game plan is all about scheme, tactics, strategic plan, strategy, tactical plan, working plan and idea also method, strategy and initiative, a strategic plan is a detailed proposal for doing or achieving a set goal or an intention or decision about what ones entire plan. This is common strategy or tactics is for attaining goals

A game plan is something that tells a leader or a professional what, how, when and why achieving particular goals. A game plan is all about taking control of the business and ensuring that others will not affect the business negatively.

A plan is a specific action which aims to help the organization or an individual in achieving its or his objectives. Every plan should have specific goals which it strives to achieve.

To write a plan is to come up with or put together a strategy by putting a great effort to achieve and develop a game plan that is more long-term-focused.

Planning Process
- Initiating; write down your goals.
- Develop goals and objectives
- Set timelines
- Actively work towards your goals
- Executing

- Monitoring and control

Initiating
The process of a game plan is to identify your strategic position and Initiate your objectives; this is the first step towards your goal achievement. Every good plan must have a beginning, write down your goals and make a formidable plan from it; initiating is the first step in starting a new goal plan. During the goal initiation phase, you establish the motive behind your goals and what you set to accomplish, Simply jotting down your goals helps to be committed to the accomplishment of the goals, it helps you to clarify exactly what you want to achieve, what your need to do daily to achieve it, goals that are written down are more powerful than goals you keep in your mind or as a dream.

Be encouraged to write a formidable and well detailed plan, the same motivation that prompted you to desire to be educated, to start your own business should be directed towards writing your goals and objectives, read more books, journals and articles, revisit all the forgotten ideas or proposals till you reach the accomplishment of your aim and purpose, Success is a product of a well-managed ideas.

Just take each day as it comes and do what you feel is right and positive you just have to take every challenge as it comes, the only person that can stop you, is you

Develop your objectives and goals
Goals can be intangible and non-measurable, but objectives are defined in terms of tangible targets. Develop it to make it feel tangible. First think carefully about what you want to achieve, and then commit to it.

Set timeline
This is a plan that shows how long a goal, plan or project will take or when it will be accomplished.

According to Cambridge dictionary, a timeline is a plan that shows the dates when the different stages of an activity or process should be completed:, a timeline can be of actions or objectives, set up a timeline for your different goals, time to start and time to accomplish them. The plan includes a timeline mapping when each step is to be accomplished.

Executing
Implementing and tracking the aim of the objectives, It is about making the whole idea work, focuses on the most important factors involved in implementation, this involves the carrying out the plans or the objectives, this is the necessary step that transforms your strategic plans into action to achieve your goals

Monitoring and control
This is an act of tracking, reviewing your progress towards accomplishing the set goals also always evaluate your performance as the plan progresses, This ensures the project remains on track, on budget and on time.
We must track our goal's progress in a way that promote transparency and accountability
Break Your Goals Into Smaller Goals. Break your goals into milestone, its like breaking them down into chapters and monitor till the end of the chapter, Reaching the next milestone in success would require hours of hard work.

Chapter 3

KEEP IN TOUCH WITH THE RIGHT PEOPLE

Keeping in touch is to continue to talk or write to someone, Try to keep in contact once or twice per week with your close friends

Socialize by participate in social activities; mix socially with others. It helps sharpen memory and cognitive skills, increases your sense of happiness and well-being,

1. ***Stay social.*** The main way a lot of people stay in touch is through social media, and it's hardly surprising when you think about the sheer number of ways we can communicate using it.

2. ***Video chats.***

Try out video calling for a face-to-face conversation. Most smartphones have video calling capabilities, which allow you to see and be seen by your friend during your conversation.

3. ***Calling***

Commit to regular phone calls. You and your friend will likely have busy schedules, but you can make plans to call each other regularly.

4. ***Regular activities.***

Teach yourselves a new skill. Learn new activities by joining clubs where like minds go to for fun or pleasure

5. ***Start a book club.***

Join a book club, read journals, articles and so on, That stack of books on your nightstand isn't going to get read unless you motivate yourself *somehow* There is a saying that "A reader lives a thousand lives before he dies . ,

Reading gives you the ability to reach higher ground. And keep climbing."–Oprah.

6. ***Attend lectures***

Attend lectures, seminars, webinars, conference, this will gives you huge opportunity to meet different types of individuals of different field, you can go to a lecture on a topic you're actually interested in *for fun* and learning.

Chapter 4

AVOID DISTRACTION

Distractions is a thing that prevents someone from concentrating on something else or extreme agitation of the mind, this may impair performance by causing multiple, distinct processes with little in common to be engaged.

Internal distractions like hunger, fatigue, illness, stress, worries, rumination other distracting thoughts can interrupt your concentration as much as external distractions.

Distractions can be external (such as noise) this may be caused by a number of factors, including the loss of interest in the primary activity, inability to pay attention due to various reasons, or intensity of the distractor.

Plenty of research has shown that distractions cause people to take longer to complete a task; they also degrade the overall quality of people's

Distractions can lead to committing twice as many errors as usual while focus increases the chances of getting the task done.

Types of distractions

Visual: taking your eyes off the roadway
Manual: taking your hands off the wheel.

Cognitive: taking your mind off driving

What are the biggest distractions?

- Mobile phone/texting
- The Internet
- Gossip
- Social media
- Media; TV, videos online
- Smoke breaks or snack breaks
- We refer to social media distraction as the phenomenon, the distractors drawing the attention away from the task at hand and directing it instead toward social media

How to Avoid Distractions and Stay Focused

- Get prepared With a To-Do List.
- Use headphone
- Stop Multitasking.
- Silence Your Phone.
- Shut off your phone
- Take on more challenging task
- Break big projects into small pieces.
- Use music and headphones to cut down noise.
- Find the best environment for efficient studying.
- Clean up and organize yourself.

Chapter 5

THINK OF POTENCIAL OBSTACLE

A difficulty or problem that prevents you from achieving something. They are real barriers to achieving a goal. We can usually do something about these and the trick is to learn how to get around these and identify the problem.
Some of the factors are;

1. *A limited or lack of finance*,
Limited finance limits purchasing power. Poor budgeting is one of the most common causes of financial problems. If a person is spending more than he is earning, he is setting himself up for money trouble or bankruptcy.

2. *Procrastination;* As the saying "procrastination is the thief of time" means if we delay to do something, it will take longer to do later on, if you observe sincerely, you will notice that everything thing you postponed or gave excuse for, you will end up not doing them

3. *Lack of will power;* willpower is a critical step to achieving that goals. At its essence, willpower is the ability to resist short-term temptations in order to meet long-term goals or is the mental ability to control yourself.

To get over this
Motivate yourself
Always think positive

Get support from others

4. Fear; One of the biggest obstacles to reaching our goals is fear. Fear is an emotion that overrides our intelligence. It stops us from moving toward our goals, this can reduce your ability to make optimal choices. Lazy peoples fear prevents them from ever making progress towards their goals.

5. Self-doubt: It makes you second-guess yourself. It demotivates you and crushes your desires.
According to dictionary, self-doubt is lack of confidence in oneself and abilities, lack of faith in oneself : a feeling of doubt or uncertainty about one's abilities, actions,

If persistent self-doubt is not addressed, it can lead to:

- Anxiety
- Depression
- lack of motivation
- Emotional instability
- Low self-esteem
- Difficulty making decisions

To Overcome

- Develop a growth mindset
- Be mindful of your thinking
- Get a professional help

6. Anxiety; Everyone has feelings of anxiety at some point in their life, Your anxiety can become a negative influence in your entire life decision making — Creating barriers in accomplishing your goals

7. Low motivation; this shows that There are no goals, desire, or willingness to work. You simply don't do anything; this can be a common symptom of depression.

Some tips to get out of Low motivation
- Continue to set new goals.
- Surround yourself with positive people
- Be Patient
- Don't question your abilities.
- Focus on the task at hand.
- Seek professional help.

8. ***Time management and constraints;*** Sometimes, finding the motivation to complete important tasks can be the first obstacle to good time management, By managing your time wisely through careful planning of every second of every day, you can control your schedule, manage your time efficiently, so that you can ultimately reach your goals.

Effective time management means getting more of the important work done in a day both efficiently and effectively, It revolves around getting more done in less time and being productive overall.

Some ways to effectively manage your time

1. Be prioritized: Rank your tasks.
2. Develop schedule.
3. Give yourself breaks
4. Continuous Improvement
5. Be focused: manage distractions.
6. Be structured: Time blocks your work.
7. Be self-aware: Track your time.
8. To-do lists and checklists.

9. Organize yourself.
10. Auditing and improving workflows.

To overcome

1. *Anticipate and identify possible obstacles*
2. *Face your challenges with courage*: you need to find the obstacles in your way and get rid of them.
3. *Take responsibility:* take control of your situations and focus on solutions that move them forward.
4. *Learn to manage time*
5. *Accept support*

Chapter 6

TRUST YOUR INTUITION

According to dictionary, intuition is the ability to understand something instinctively, without the need for conscious reasoning. To trust one's intuition is to follow your instinct, this can help you in accurate decisions making and gives you more confidence, but it can be dangerously unreliable in complicated situations, it's a thoughts drop into your mind from nowhere

Following your instinct can certainly direct you toward the best path for achieving your goals, your intuition helps you make decisions quickly and allows you to adapt to rapidly changing conditions

Self-trust comes from listening to your intuition; *trust* in *your intuition* is an important way to build sustainable confidence in yourself. It simply comes naturally and with no judgment. You can rely or base your judgment on intuition.

There are types of intuition thinking;
Emotional
Spiritual
Mental

You can naturally more intuitive if you are creative and imaginative, smart and passionate.

Chapter 7

PERSONAL DEVELOPMENT

Skill developmental goals are objectives and target you set to improve your behavior, skills and capabilities. Setting these goals involves critical assessment of yourself and identifying the areas in which you need improvement to maximize your potential and abilities, the first thing you need to check is your total performance

Check your total performance

In other for capacities to be maximized, you need to do a self-performance review, you should first determine where you are in your professional career since the last reviewed, you need to do a self-evaluation, Self-evaluation is very essential in determine your overall success both in short and long term aspirations.

Provide a precise measure to help access your work. Encourage yourself to be more strategic in their approach to achieving your goal.

It's important that self-ratings are aligned with the feedback you've gotten from your last self-evaluation, a personal development objective could be about developing a specific skill or behaviour, or increasing your knowledge in a particular area.

The following key points will guide you in checking your performance:

- Make a list of your positive attributes.
- Develop your personal vision
- Reflect on your accomplishments.
- Reflect on your mistakes.
- Areas of accomplishment since last review.
- Insights on productivity.
- Areas of improvement since last review.
- Growth plan or professional development plan.
- Personal values.
- Develop a reading habit.
- Learn new things.
- Work with a coach or mentor to assemble a plan.
- Increase professional knowledge and training

Importance of personal development

Being committed to personal development helps you to become more focused. It helps you to resist distractions without needing to have deadlines constantly

Personal development is a lifelong process. It is a way for people to assess their skills and qualities, consider their aims in life and set goals in order to realize and maximize their potential. it can help you explore where to make improvements in your life.

Chapter 8

WORK ON YOUR MINDSET

Your *mindset* is your collection of thoughts and beliefs that shape your thought habits. This in turn affects your thought habits and personality; it is a person's way of thinking and their opinions

Work on your mindset, be positive and confident, our chances for success may often lie simply within our mindset.

The state of your mindset influences how you think, feel, and behave in any given situation and your chances for success may often lie simply within your mindset. Always believe you will succeed in life or reach your desired goals.

What you need to do;

Identify Your Mindset. Your mindset can influence your ability to learn, grow, and achieve your goals, peoples mindsets are constantly shifting and changing, so there is need for you to identify the kind of mindset, whether its fixed or growth.
Once you've identified your top negative and bad thoughts, you need to develop a way to stop them from holding you back or be hindrance to your success

Face your fears. According to dictionary.com, fear is a distressing emotion aroused by impending danger, evil, pain, etc., whether the threat is real or imagined; the feeling or condition of being afraid.

These could be;

1. ***Fear of failure;*** The fear of failure, which is sometimes referred to as atychiphobia, it's an intense fear of non-fulfillment and this can lead to emotional problems and eventually leads to depression.

2. ***Anxiety;*** these can actually become problems if it's not well taking care of, it causes harm to your physical and mental stability

3. ***Fear of the future;*** We cannot avoid being fearful of future for as long as we are alive, but staying fearful will reduce your ability of a good decision, and also to think big and create value in your life.
To overcome our fears; We must identify our fear and understudy it

Meditation, Meditation for Success, Confidence and Self-Esteem, The power of meditation creates ideas, this is pondering on your written goals, on your aspirations, Build yourself up with positive thinking, spend a few minutes with meditating positively and make it all about you. Also be passionate (love what you are doing) Positive energy and efforts are one of the most effective motivating factors, praise yourself for achieving an ultimate goal or for accomplished milestones along the way. Just take each day as it comes and do what you feel is right and positive, you just have to take every challenge as it comes, just note that the only person that can stop you is you.

The power of positive thinking can be achieved, find your inspiration and motivation every day, your mindsets will play a significant role in determining life's outcomes.

Believe the time is now and focus on your long-term vision.

Trust your intuition, According to dictionary, intuition is the

ability to understand something instinctively, without the need for conscious reasoning. to trust one's intuition is to follow your instinct, this can help you in accurate decisions making and gives you more confidence, but it can be dangerously unreliable in complicated situations
Its a Thoughts drop into your mind from nowhere

There are types of intuition thinking;
Emotional
Spiritual
Mental

Chapter 9

LEARN FROM YOUR MISTAKES

Success provides us great fulfilment and satisfaction, as attaining success means getting the thing that we desire and aspire.

"The road to success is paved with failure." Failure can show us our deficiency and limitations or goal and allow us to try to change that and to improve ourselves. It can also show us what does work and what we should keep doing

However, each failure along that journey is likely to be unique. Most likely, success is attained through a variety of attempts (and failures).

We can gain so much knowledge from our mistakes, and all it takes is the willingness to learn from them, there is a saying that, "The only man who never makes a mistake is the man who never does anything"

Ways to learn from mistakes

- Acknowledge your mistakes. When you make a mistake, try to admit it as soon as you can, and apologize if necessary.
- Analyze your mistakes
- Consider mistakes as opportunities
- Do not let your mistakes define you.
- Let go of the fear of failure.
- Reshape your goals.
- View Mistakes as Opportunities.

Identify the skills, knowledge, resources, or tools that will keep you from repeating the error; In fact, learning from failure is often the key to success. By getting things wrong, you'll improve your skills and grow in various ways. The only man who never makes a mistake is the man who never does anything

Having experienced failure pushes you to go after your dreams. It teaches you to keep trying and trying until you get it right. This is what eventually leads to success.

Chapter 10

BE INNOVATIVE

Be innovative (create ideas) learn to doing things differently, be innovative from your thought, think or generate ideas and solutions to challenges or problems, use logic and creativity to overcome the problems, also develop the ability to come up with new ideas and develop approaches to problems

According to Oxford Living Dictionaries, creativity is defined as "the use of imagination or original ideas to create something." Innovation, on the other hand, means "a new method, idea, and product.

This is enhancing creativity using individual problem-solving skills in creating and implementing new ideas, innovative It's a result. It's an outcome and becomes a product

Ways of being innovative;

Have bank of ideas. This contains a whole list of ideas that you can pull out and touch up when you need them,

Broaden your scope, or extend, widen or expand, your horizon through knowledge and experience; through reasoning, listening and socializing, increase the range of your knowledge, understanding and experience.

Surround yourself with inspiration and bring them to life; when you surround yourself with positive influences, it becomes that much easier to stay focused on your end goals, surrounding yourself with people who lift you up, lend you knowledge, and help you learn from mistakes, you need to surround yourself with people who will help you achieve your goals

Be creative, imaginative, inventive, original, and innovational, all you think of is find new ways to do things. To be imaginative is to be inventive and original.

Be proactive, be action oriented, don't leave what you can do today for tomorrow, do not procrastinate, be constantly processing information, this makes new ideas and innovations unchallenging.

Develop Communication skills, this involves listening, speaking, observing, direct manner, using easily understood language, a good communication is when a sender sends a message to the receiver and he received it with understanding, communicating in a clear, effective and efficient way is an extremely special and useful skill.

3 Communication skills used on daily basis including:

1. Verbal: Communicating by way of a spoken language, an oral communication, If we have strong verbal communication skills, we are more likely to experience success, it makes people want to listen to you

2. Written: Communicating by way of written language, symbols and numbers

3. Nonverbal: Communicating by way of body language or facial expressions.

Conclusion

Success is an accomplishment, achievement, success always looks ahead of the lame excuses and puts itself forward than the created misconceptions; Success is the result of key determination and concentration while moving ahead in the path of workings.

The story of all the ten world-renowned personalities is enough to motivates us towards reaching the goal of success.
Accomplishing goals is possible, by practicing the principles that you have just learned from this book, you will move to the front of the line in life. You will have an incredible advantage over people who do not know or who do not practice these techniques and strategies. By setting goals, we ensure ourselves a certain level of motivation and desire each day.

Be determined to continue regardless of how difficult the circumstances.

I wish you Good luck on starting a brand new chapter in your life and hope that you will accomplish even more, all the best.

www.ingramcontent.com/pod-product-compliance
Lightning Source LLC
Chambersburg PA
CBHW050308220526
45465CB00002B/874